# THE SEVEN LAST WORDS OF CHRIST

# + Jesus, Keep Me Near the Cross

Jesus, keep me near the cross,
There a precious fountain,
Free to all, a healing stream,
Flows from Calv'ry's mountain.

REFRAIN:

In the cross, in the cross
Be my glory ever,
Till my raptured soul shall find
Rest beyond the river.

Near the cross, a trembling soul,
Love and mercy found me;
There the Bright and Morning Star
Sheds its beams around me.
(REFRAIN)

Near the cross! O Lamb of God,
Bring its scenes before me;
Help me walk from day to day
With its shadows o'er me.
(REFRAIN)

Near the cross I'll watch and wait,
Hoping, trusting ever,
Till I reach the golden strand
Just beyond the river.

REFRAIN:

In the cross, in the cross
Be my glory ever,
Till my raptured soul shall find
Rest beyond the river.

*Fanny J. Crosby, 1820–1915*

JUDITH
MATTISON

# THE SEVEN LAST WORDS OF CHRIST

## The Message of the Cross
for Today

Augsburg
MINNEAPOLIS

THE SEVEN LAST WORDS OF CHRIST
The Message of the Cross for Today

Interior design: James F. Brisson
Cover design: Lecy Design
Cover photo: *Via Dolorosa,* Jerusalem. Historical Pictures/Stock Montage

Mattison, Judith
    The seven last words of Christ : the message of the cross for today / Judith Mattison.
        p.    cm.
    ISBN 0-8066-2628-3
    1. Jesus Christ—Seven last words—Meditations. I. Title.
BT456.M388   1992
232.96'35—dc20                                                    92-19355
                                                                      CIP

The paper used in this publication meets the minimum requirements of American National Standard for Information Sciences—Permanence of Paper for Printed Library Materials, ANSI Z329.48-1984.          ∞ ™

Manufactured in the U.S.A.                                     AF 9-2628
08    07    06    05              13    14    15    16    17    18

*This book is dedicated with love
to my mentor and friend*
THE REVEREND STANLEY SANDBERG
*He has loved the church and served Christ
with grace and wisdom.*

*In the early sixties I sat in the pews of Emanuel Lutheran
Church in Hartford, Connecticut, Sunday after Sunday listening to its pastor, the Reverend Stanley Sandberg, preach
with skill and conviction. His words opened doors of faith to
me which I had never before encountered. I began to take
notes on the sermons. I learned marvelous hymns; and I can
still hear Pastor Sandberg dismissing us, after the recessional
hymn, with a benediction from Jude. Those experiences were
the beginning of my journey toward ordination. Over the
years, Stanley has continued to support and encourage me,
gently nudging my understandings with his knowledge and
his dry humor. It is to him that this book is affectionately
dedicated.*

# CONTENTS

*T* *he seven last words of Christ are gathered from the accounts of Good Friday in all
four Gospels. They provide us an opportunity
to focus on the cross and on how Jesus understood and expressed his sacrifice of dying for
our sins. This volume has one meditation on
each word, as well as poetry, hymns, and other
materials that enlarge the possible meanings
of each word.*

# + Sacrifice

The Good Father
Carries his son up the hill,
Bending over him,
Heavy with sorrow and tears.
The path is ragged,
The Father worn weary
By the long struggle of
Knowing hate and rejection.
He carries his only child
Knowing
The child is the only gift
Great enough to ransom
Those he would protect and love.
Against the clouded sky
He raises up his own
To experience and overcome
The cross.

FIRST WORD

# "Father, forgive them."

LUKE 23:34

# ✝ Complicity

A group of friends sat together talking after dinner one evening. Conversation turned to a recent news story. A man in a neighboring county allegedly killed a man, mutilating the body afterward. One of the group had great difficulty handling the reality of such violence, asking, "How could anybody do such a thing?"

In another situation a couple went to a marriage counselor. The husband had confessed to his wife that he had once had an affair. His wife was angry and hurt about the betrayal. "I would *never* do that to him!" she said emphatically.

In such bold cases of transgression, it's hard to believe we are capable of the same errors, the same folly. We have better images of ourselves. We have standards, ethics. We have made promises and commitments that we intend to keep. We cannot imagine ourselves capable of murder. And therein lies the tale of our human sin, our frailty, our attempts to persuade ourselves that we are God.

Probably all of us have sat in a worship service, listening to a sermon and earnestly hoping that someone else sitting nearby is hearing the message because that someone "really needs to hear this." Somehow we imagine that we're the people in the white hats and clean gloves. It's other folks who need correction. Peter did it too. He quarreled with Jesus when his Master told him that Peter would deny Jesus three times. "No way!" Peter argued. "I'm a believer. I love you, Lord! It can't happen to me!"

However, we all know that it *did* happen to Peter. Even loyal, enthusiastic Peter denied his Lord and was devastated to realize his humanness.

Life is about being human. Life, as exciting and wonderful as it is, is about being sinners—people who let each other down, people who fail. We live in the tension of an imperfect world, the tension of our own frailty. We try to shore up ourselves with walls of self-acclaim or lists of our good deeds or fantasies of being superhuman. Ultimately we fail. As we look honestly at the sin in our world we know that there, but for the grace of God, are we—people capable of hate and anger. We are people who kid ourselves if we think we will not be tempted by the appeal of a lust-filled relationship. We all are people who fall short of the glory of God, as Paul reminds us.

Actually, Paul can be a great help to us in this struggle. In his early years he was a champion when it came to self-righteousness and highlighting other people's sin. Paul was a champion at noticing the log in everyone else's eye and path . . . until he met the Holy Spirit of God on a path to Damascus. When Paul met Jesus, he knew: Paul was a heavy-duty sinner. He was capable of murder and lust and self-righteousness and the rejection of God. We all are. We're human beings.

Of course, we try not to know the depth of our dark side. It's very difficult and frightening to imagine that our anger could overcome us to the point of destroying another life. We even overlook how our careless words destroy the lives and dreams of those we love in our families or of those we work and play with. We don't like to know because we don't like to be condemned. Of course! The Law is hard. The Law is relentless in its condemnation of our thoughts, words, and deeds. We are in bondage to our human struggles, to our sin; and we are afraid we are unforgivable. We deny our weakness, our culpability, because we are unable to imagine that God can forgive such as we. We try not to know our dark side because we fear that the sunlight of forgiveness would never shine on us. We stand at the foot of the cross and see only the darkening sky, the death, the misery. Jesus is dying and we with him because it is, after all, our fault.

> Who was the guilty?
> Who brought this upon thee?
> ................................
> I it was denied thee.
> I crucified thee.
>
> *AH, HOLY JESUS*

The pain of the crucifixion for every one of us is that we are the ones who caused it to happen. We have tried to locate the responsibility and guilt in other characters in the drama, but we are the ones. We are they. We did it.

We blame the Pharisees. They badgered Jesus about the Sabbath and about his claims of authority. They were so "right" in their liturgies and rules that they destroyed human compassion and the dreams of the faithful. They could not allow Jesus or any person to suggest that all of us are equal sinners before God. We blame the Pharisees for Jesus' death.

We blame Pilate, symbol of law and order and the government. He had the power to change the outcome, but he did not follow his personal conviction. He caved in to the pressure of special interests and his own ambition. We blame Pilate for killing Jesus.

We are horrified by the violence of the soldiers. The soldiers beat Jesus and mocked him and lost their ability to feel the suffering that Jesus experienced. We blame the soldiers.

But God knows we are the Pharisees. We are those who kill the dreams of people by crushing their spirits and lives with rules that do not give life but destroy it. We hear and see Jesus drawing into the circle of love all the riffraff and victims of this hostile world. We don't like it. We don't like diversity or change.

And we are like Pilate, silent in the struggle against oppression, overlooking the pain of those who live without hope because we prefer our comfort. We feed the hungry only enough to salve our consciences and keep land and resources for ourselves. And we are the soldiers, for humanity dies every single day at the hands of those who choose violence over peace. In some cases, we pay them to do our destruction for us. In everyday terms, we destroy peace by gossip and retaliation. We do not turn the other cheek; we slap it and run away. We hate the thought, but we kill Jesus every day in the way we live. We are in bondage to sin and cannot do otherwise.

Today we must come to terms with our complicity. Today we stand before the cross as the skies grow dark and the Son of the only God hangs dying. We weep with Peter because we remember times when we changed the subject as people began to talk about religion. We remember other times when we said, "They're nice enough people, but they don't fit in with us. They'd feel out of place and never be happy in our group anyway."

Today we cannot simply notice our own faults in others and ignore them in ourselves. The sight of the innocent Son of God hanging on a cross forces us to come to terms with our own personal, daily, repeated faults and injustices. It's hard to face up to the Law this way. We hate its condemnation. But we cannot hide or run away. Today we acknowledge that we are modern-day self-righteous Pharisees. Like the soldiers of Pilate we are calloused by the pain of the world, and we rationalize our hardened hearts.

Yet the sight of the cross changes things. Even the centurion—a soldier—knew: this was surely the Son of God. We know it too. It is in that moment of realization that our world changes. The relentless pursuit of the law which condemns us is set aside. The conviction of our sinful selves is shattered. Right here, as we look up at the cross of pain and abuse and broken compassion, we see the Savior saying something. His lips form the words which all Pharisees and soldiers and sinners for all time must hear.

"Father," says Jesus, "forgive them." Like a morning after a rainstorm our tension is broken and lifted away. We are sinners. We own our complicity. But we are not forsaken or abandoned. We are held in the hand of God's grace. We are capable of great sin, and we have been wrong. But we are forgivable and we are loved.

"Father, forgive them. . . ."

God can and does forgive us. Thanks be to God for this inexpressible gift!

## To Consider

1. What actions, such as using violence against someone else, do I tend to think I am incapable of doing?

2. How does acknowledging our sins bring us closer to God?

3. How have I been callous to the world's needs?

4. Whom have I "killed" in some way or excluded or harmed? Do I sometimes hurt others and not know what I am doing? From Jesus' first word from the cross, what can I learn about forgiveness?

5. Remembering a time when someone forgave us can help us realize what Jesus' words mean. How did I feel when that happened to me? How did it change my thinking about that person?

6. What people are waiting for my forgiveness of them? What is holding me back?

# + Ah, Holy Jesus

Ah, holy Jesus, how hast thou offended
That man to judge thee hath in hate pretended?
By foes derided, by thine own rejected,
O most afflicted.

Who was the guilty? Who brought this upon thee?
Alas, my treason, Jesus, hath undone thee.
'Twas I, Lord Jesus, I it was denied thee;
I crucified thee.

*Johann Heermann, 1585–1647;*
*trans. Robert Bridges, 1844–1930, altered*

## + Killing Jesus

I imagine that I
would never be the one
who tried to kill Jesus.
My retrospective view
convinces me I'm loyal.
Yet I kill him every day
  by ignoring others
  worshiping power
  idolizing upward mobility
  resisting sharing
  harboring self-hatred
and being too busy
to read God's Word.
Most of all, if I admit
that Jesus is God's heir,
I must be dependent on him.
I would have to change myself.
I'd rather let him die.

*Walking the Way*
Fortress Press 1986
© Judith Mattison

## + Father, Forgive Them

It was to the Romans
that Jesus spoke forgiveness—
they who had humiliated him publicly
and beaten his body.
And he spoke to religious leaders.
Certainly they had done all they could
to undermine his ministry:
they had spoiled the Temple
and self-righteously claimed privilege over compassion.
Jesus spoke to the disciples
who seemed never to understand his purpose
and both betrayed and denied him.

But Jesus did not speak to government and religious leaders,
nor even to his followers only.
He spoke to us:
we who ignore the call to sacrifice for others,
we who prefer our self-concern,
we who hate to change
and who destroy the earth and each other
in small pieces.
It is to us he spoke —
Father, forgive them:
for they know not what they do.

SECOND WORD

"Today you will be
with me in Paradise."

LUKE 23:43

# ✝ The Unexpected

A high school class gathered for its twenty-five-year reunion. People had looked forward to this summer event. Several had been on diets. Some bought new dresses or shoes or ties. Classmates tucked photos of their families into their pockets and headed for a large downtown hotel.

Once there, noises of surprise and happiness filled the hall. But there were awkward moments. One of the worst was when a classmate came up with a big grin and said, "Remember me?" It was a terrifying moment because people change. Bodies were larger or slimmer, hair color had changed, hair had receded or disappeared altogether. Twenty-five years had dimmed memories. There the person stood, expecting to be identified. It was embarrassing—and impossible to tell who had asked, "Remember me?"

Later, people gathered in small groups, comparing experiences and remembering friends. One man had become prominent in his field. "Well!" said a classmate. "Isn't that something! He certainly was no angel in college!" And so it went. A summer evening of fun and gossip and remembering, a reunion.

Let's go back to the astonished response of a classmate when told of the success of another. "Well! He certainly was no angel in college!" The implication was that this man hadn't deserved or earned his good fortune. Interesting, isn't it, how we question whether people deserve their success? We express it in phrases like, "Did she get a good break?" or "He's lucky, considering his attitude," or "Can you believe it? She never worked a day in her life!"

When we interpret the events of life in that way, it simplifies our thinking. Things work out evenly, predictably. We try to live by worldly mottos: "You get what you deserve." "Crime doesn't pay." "The guys in the white hats win." "Hard work always pays off." "The innocent will be set free." We often transfer those formulas to our understanding of theology: If you have troubles now, then you must have sinned earlier. Or we believe that when you are virtuous, God will bless your life with good things. Or we hold the classic colonial American belief that when people are wealthy, it is a sign that they're "better" than other people. There are many indications that people still hold those opinions today. The ways of the world have tidy answers to life. According to those maxims, life is very fair. No wonder Job had a lot of trouble fitting his unhappy circumstances into the mottos of the world. He didn't seem to deserve to have problems. He'd been a good person. It wasn't fair.

Throughout Jesus' ministry he taught us that our ways of thinking and acting are not God's ways. "The last shall be first," he warned, to their astonishment. In a parable Jesus told us about the owner of a vineyard who paid latecomers as much as those who worked all day! These are not the rules of the world.

Then on Good Friday, on a cross alongside Jesus, a thief embodied that contrast between the world's rules and God's. He told another criminal, "We are getting what we deserve for our deeds, but this man [Jesus] has done nothing wrong." The thief recognized the injustice in Jesus' execution. A thief like himself deserved condemnation. Not Jesus.

Then the thief did something amazing. He said, "Jesus, remember me when you come into your kingdom." It was a statement of belief—not from a disciple but from a criminal. Those we might have expected to stand by Jesus through hard times left him. Fiercely loyal Peter denied knowing him. Others hid away in fear. Who spoke of Jesus and his kingdom? A thief!

The passion story is filled with characters who do the unexpected. Disciples fall asleep. The enemies who are responsible for the death of this rabbi Son of God are not the Romans but the Jews. At their insistence, a ruthless highwayman goes free and a mild-mannered teacher is killed. And who calls Jesus the Messiah, the Son of God? Not his friends and supporters. No. It is Pilate who nails the title *King of the Jews* to his cross. It is a Roman soldier who confesses, "Truly this man was God's Son!" (Mark 15:39).

As always, God's ways are not our ways. God speaks and acts through whomever God chooses. On one hand Pilate lives by the world's rules. Finding Jesus innocent, he arranges events into an exercise of weights and balances. He sentences Jesus but frees Barabbas. Even so, God chooses to use Pilate as the one to name Jesus king.

And what Jew would ever have imagined that the promised Messiah of God would die? It was diametrically contrary to all their expectations of the Messiah coming in glory to establish the kingdom of the people of Israel. The disciples refused to believe the predictions of Jesus regarding his death. Peter tried to prevent Jesus from saying it. It was unbelievable and frightening. They—and we—are always surprised by God, whose ways are not our ways.

"Jesus," said the condemned thief, "remember me when you come into your kingdom." It's ironic: the disciples hid. The religious leaders scoffed. But it was the repentant thief who pleaded for forgiveness.

Did the thief deserve forgiveness? Not by worldly standards. In life, isn't it true that we get what we deserve? If we sin now, we pay later, right? Crime doesn't pay. The innocent go free and the white hats win. According to the world, the thief deserves condemnation, deserves death.

To our chagrin and amazement, the Messiah dies and the thief is told, "Truly I tell you, today you will be with me in Paradise." Once again we are startled. The last *are* first! God does it again. The laborers are paid the same, even for

25

different work contributions. What kind of way is that to run a business?

It's God's way, and thank God for it. For, although we don't always want to acknowledge it, *we* deserve to die. We certainly aren't angels either. We are insensitive and self-centered, and self-righteous. There is a dark side in all of us that we keep carefully hidden or covered by virtuous acts. We don't care to expose our true nature. If the truth be known, we deserve to die.

We deserve to die, but we can be like the thief. We can repent. We can plead to the Savior that we also may be welcomed into the kingdom. And with the death and resurrection of Jesus, we will live. At the Great Reunion in eternity, we will be remembered! We won't deserve it. We can't be good enough to earn it. Our wealth is not an indication of our virtue or goodness. Indeed, it may be quite the opposite. But when we who must die to this life say, "Jesus, remember me," he will. Even from the cross he promises us that for God, death is not the final word. "Today," he says, "you will be with me in Paradise."

Thanks be to God!

# To Consider

1. Have I ever been surprised when someone succeeded in life whom I thought would fail? When have I been able to do something I thought I couldn't do?

2. Who are those whom I assume will be "last"? Does any person or group think of me as "last"?

3. What situations in the world do I see that I think are unfair?

4. Do I sometimes think some people deserve the calamities that happen to them?

5. When have God's ways not been my ways? How do I know, or can I know, what God's ways are?

6. What do we deserve? And what, thanks to God's action through Jesus, do we get?

## + Remember

Please, Lord, remember.
Remember me as
  the child you made
  born fresh, loving
  open to life and people.
Forget
  my mistakes
  my selfish behavior
  my stubborn will
  my silent hate.
You have created and named me.
  I have fallen away.
Love me back to you, Lord.
Remember my sins and misdeeds
  no more.
Lead me in your forgiven Way.

*Walking the Way*
Fortress Press 1986
© Judith Mattison

# + Wide Open Are Your Hands

Wide open are your hands to pay with more than gold
The awful debt of guilt and sin, forever and of old.
Ah, let me grasp those hands, that we may never part,
And let the power of their blood sustain my fainting heart.

Wide open are your arms, a fallen world to embrace,
To win to love and endless rest our wayward human race.
Lord, I am sad and poor, but boundless is your grace;
Give me the soul-transforming joy for which I seek your face.

*Attributed to Bernard of Clairvaux, 1091–1153;*
*trans. Charles Porterfield Krauth, 1823–1883, altered*

THIRD WORD

# "Woman, behold, your son!"
# "Behold, your mother!"

JOHN 19:26-27 (RSV)

# ✝ Family Love

Whthen the cry of a newborn baby stirs the air, it is totally new. This sound has never been heard before. This is a beginning. The baby is placed in the mother's arms, and bonding begins. This is also true when a parent first holds an adopted baby. Bonding begins in the embrace of arms around the child. A new relationship is formed.

It must have been that way for Mary, the mother of Jesus. She carried her baby for nine months. She felt the peculiar rolling movement of arms and legs across her tightened abdomen. She felt the child within her as she awkwardly rode a donkey into Bethlehem for the census. She had been told this child would be unique. She may have wondered about that, but she no doubt experienced the curiosity, discomfort, and ultimately the birth pangs that all new mothers experience. She began to bond with him before she ever saw him. This was to be her son.

Then the baby came, and his voice must have stirred the air as never before, joining the angel's chorus. Mary held him and pondered all the excitement and unusual events that happened those days. She kept them in her heart.

Jesus was born to a family—a poor, laboring family of no particular reputation, of no pretense. Although we have little

NOTE: *It is dangerous to assume, or to project from our imaginations, the feelings or unspoken thoughts of people in Scripture. Often we cannot substantiate our assumptions. However, I have taken that liberty in the opening paragraphs of this meditation. I trust you will take that into account as you consider its effectiveness or usefulness for you.*

information about his formative years, we sense that he experienced a childhood of security and good religious education in a contented family.

Still, when Jesus began his ministry at age thirty, he surrounded himself with disciples and friends; and they became the focal point of his life and mission. Again and again they asked him about his intentions, his purpose, his relationship to God, whom he called Daddy—Abba. "Who are you?" they wondered.

"Who do you say that I am?" Jesus countered (Mark 8:29).

"Are you the one who is to come, or are we to wait for another?" John the Baptist asked him (Luke 7:20). And one Sabbath day his astonished listeners asked, "Where did this man get all this? What is the wisdom that has been given to him? What deeds of power are being done by his hands! Is not this the carpenter, the son of Mary and brother of James and Joses and Judas and Simon, and are not his sisters here with us?"

Jesus replied that a prophet is not without honor except in his own country and among his own kin and in his own house (Mark 6:2-4).

Earlier in Mark, Jesus asked the significant question, "Who are my mother and my brothers?" He then answered himself by saying, "Whoever does the will of God is my brother and sister and mother" (Mark 3:33, 35). The meaning of family was stretched beyond birth order and bloodlines and traditional definitions of family to include all believers. Jesus expanded the already broad Jewish concept of extended social family to include all believers. All people were to be bound, bonded in the family of God.

But the years ahead brought disruption to the disciples and followers of Jesus. By Good Friday nearly all had run from him, denied him, abandoned their friend and Savior. Jesus was alone. Then came Mary and John, the beloved friend of Jesus. Jesus was stirred by this sight. He assigned to each of them an ongoing relationship based not on bloodlines but on love.

"Woman," he told Mary, indicating John, "behold your son." And to John he said, "Behold your mother" (John 19:26-27 RSV).

We expect a great deal from our families. Robert Frost wrote, "Home is the place where, when you have to go there, they have to take you in" (*Mending Wall*, 1914). For many, family means the people we were raised with, those with whom we have been honest, those who accept us, who live with us and understand us even without words or explanations. For others, family has been people unrelated to us genetically, people who were surrogate parents, friends who replaced brothers or sisters, aunts, uncles, grandparents. In those situations, the bond that holds us together is love and commitment rather than birth or housing. These are the family members who take us in by choice not chance.

Jesus, hanging alone on the cross, saw below him two of those people in his life who were bound to him by love and who stayed with him, committed, even in the hours of his dying. Mary and John, beloved ones, stayed through his pain in loyalty and compassion. As Jesus spoke to them, he redefined their understanding of family. Woman, your son. Friend, she is now your mother.

In this poignant moment Jesus gave us a new understanding of family. Family is more than genetic. Think over your life experience. Are there those who have nurtured you as a parent might have done? Are there those who remembered you on special occasions and listened to you when you felt discouraged? You may have said of a friend, "He's like the brother I never had." In your lifetime, has someone stayed beside you through illness or betrayal? Such people accept us as we are, overlooking our petulance and forgiving our slights of selfishness. These people become our family by their presence of love, their loyalty and patience and compassion.

For Christians, family also goes beyond normal limitations to include all people as our brothers and sisters. God has taken a world of disparate cultures and experiences and pulled it into unity in the person of Jesus. "Whoever does the will of God is my brother and sister and mother." We feed not only our toddlers in the high chair but those who hunger in Somalia and Brazil as well. Behold your son.

We embrace all classes of people—those like us, those of wealth, those of poverty. We do not set aside and cast away the aged ones. We remember and care for them all. "Friend, behold, she is your mother now."

How do we do all these things? From what source do we get the energy and compassion to take in all people as part of the family? We are sustained and motivated by the parent God with whom we have been bonded since we were in our mother's womb. This God embraces us in our first cry, bonded to us in love and protection. There is no power on earth that can separate us from the love of God in Christ Jesus. Jesus has walked the road of suffering alongside us, and God welcomes us home after our painful journeys.

From the cross Jesus speaks the blessing of family to all who might otherwise feel alone in the world. We are brothers and sisters, parents and children in Christ. Behold your mothers. Behold your sons. Behold your Savior, Jesus the Christ, son of the living God. Welcome to the family.

# To Consider

1. Are my expectations of my personal family unrealistically high? What are my expectations of my church family?

2. In addition to my family, who has nurtured me and served as a family member in my life? What qualities did that person have?

3. Who are the ones I could nurture and welcome as though they were family to me?

4. How do I feel when others do not stand up for me? How do I feel about myself when I don't stand up for one of my family members or a friend?

5. When are we likely to feel comfortable and happy about including other people in our churches or groups? When are we likely to feel uncomfortable?

## + Even from the Cross

Even from the cross
Jesus was caring for us.
He knew we need a parent's love.
He knew we need the young
to tend to us in our old age.
And Jesus knew we can be loved
by people other than our family.
Our friends, our neighbors,
even strangers
can be our family of love.
Even from the cross
he took care of us:
"Woman, behold your son.
Behold, your mother."

## + Family

The boy's relatives abandoned him by
ignoring his needs,
mocking differences,
leaving tears drying on his cheeks
unheeded.
He was alone.
A friend from school
brought him home for supper,
a warm kitchen
and people who smiled at him
and didn't seem to notice
if he wasn't perfect.
They even helped him
as he cleaned up his spilled milk.
He visited often,
kindergarten to junior high,
then a basketball player, tall and strong.
At graduation he kissed each one,
for they were his family,
and the mother gently held him,
her handkerchief drying the tears
which dripped from his happy eyes.

"Behold, your son."

## + Blest Be the Tie That Binds

Blest be the tie that binds our hearts in Christian love;
The unity of heart and mind is like to that above.

Before our Father's throne we pour our ardent prayers;
Our fears, our hopes, our aims are one, our comforts and our
cares.

We share our mutual woes, our mutual burdens bear,
And often for each other flows the sympathizing tear.

From sorrow, toil, and pain, and sin we shall be free;
And perfect love and friendship reign through all eternity.

*John Fawcett, 1740–1817, altered*

FOURTH WORD

# "My God, My God, why have you forsaken me?"

MARK 15:34

# ✝ My God, Why?

A young woman crouched in the corner of the pastor's office. She wore a blue bandana on her tousled long brown hair, blue jeans, and a plain blouse. She wept as she related her story of abandonment. A man she trusted and with whom she had traveled cross-country had left her, driven away from her as if she had no meaning to him. She was absolutely destitute in a strange city. No friends. No money. No hope. The wail of her cracking voice resounded through the room, was carried far beyond us, and tore the fabric of the air. "Why do I live?" she cried out and moaned. "Why do I live!"

Hers was despair. Utter desolation. In that moment her life had no meaning and no future. She felt alone and helpless, betrayed and frightened. Despair: separation from the life-giving God. Despair: feeling forsaken by the one who created us. It is as the psalmist cried out, "My God, my God, why have you forsaken me? Why are you so far from helping me, from the words of my groaning? O my God, I cry by day, but you do not answer; and by night, but find no rest" (Ps. 22:1-2).

When pain shuddered through Jesus' body and his eyes were blurred with the shock of the cross, he cried out those words: "My God, my God, why have you forsaken me?" (Matt. 27:46, Mark 15:34). Despair engulfed him as he, too, felt alone and helpless, betrayed and frightened. In that fully human moment, he doubted the constancy of God. He had no future. He felt abandoned.

41

You and I experience such moments of despair. Whether or not we express it in words, we cry out as Jesus and the woman in the pastor's office did: "My God! Why?" Why does our child become ill or use drugs? Why did we lose our job? Why did we get passed by in the selection process? Why did our friend die? Why must we have arthritis or cancer? Why? Where are you, God, in the midst of my pain and trouble? Despair. If God is faithful and good, why do we suffer? Are we forsaken?

Part of our frustration can be traced to our modern human desire to attribute cause-and-effect relationships to all events. If he doesn't brush his teeth, then he'll get cavities. She got a ticket because she was speeding. In our tidy way we want everything to add up.

One expression of that cause-and-effect description of life is crime and punishment. Sin now; pay later. We run into trouble when problems happen to us. "What have we done to deserve this?" we protest. Or at times we observe people, whom we would describe as "very good" people, besieged with problems and pain. Why must they suffer? we wonder. Nobody has that much pain coming. Things are not fair! Have they sinned so badly? The cause-and-effect principle seems to be askew.

Place alongside those examples this example: The sinless one, Jesus Christ himself, who had done nothing wrong, was dying on a cross in humiliation. He ached throughout his flesh. He bled. He thirsted. He was in agony. And he had done nothing wrong. This is supremely unfair. No cause-and-effect principles apply. Jesus despaired at the very core of his being. "Why? Why, God?"

Jesus despaired because Jesus was one of us. He was fully human, a man who walked freely into our human story. Hear the verses of Psalm 22 as they describe his plight: "Yea, dogs are round about me; a company of evildoers encircle me; they have pierced my hands and feet—I can count all my bones— they stare and gloat over me; they divide my garments among them, and for my raiment they cast lots" (Ps. 22:16-18 RSV). He felt what the woman in the pastor's office felt. No one cared anymore. Everyone had left her. She had no hope and no future. Jesus understood her because Jesus had experienced the same. More than that, there was no simple formula to point to in order to justify *why* he had to experience this tragedy. No reason. No known cause. It was grossly unfair.

We experience despair, separation from God, because we are human beings who sin. It is not a neat pattern where a particular, measurable level of sin leads to an equal, measurable punishment. But we are caught in all the sin of humanity. From the moment we rebelled and tried to take life into our own hands, we were separated from God. Like a fault in the crust of the earth, we stood on the edge of a precipice that kept us from being in touch with our life-giving Creator. We could not, and we cannot, reach across the fault line to touch God. It is too far.

We are too entangled in the complexities of our own selfishness and our corporate bondage to sin. We realize the magnitude of our spoiled world, how our sin has led to hunger and sickness and hate and death. At those moments we despair. How can we make things good? The world will never perfect itself. We will always have pain because we always choose sin and separation over God. This is despair. Hopelessness. We are terrified that we will never find God.

But wait! See how Jesus hangs in despair, calling out the very words of Psalm 22. Like the psalmist, he is pleading, "Why are you so far from helping me?" (22:1). Then, a change. "Those who seek him shall praise the Lord. . . . All the ends of the earth shall remember and turn to the Lord" (22:26-27). The man on the cross has reached across the precipice to us— to *us*! He despairs, his voice an echo of our own. In his cry we hear and see that God truly understands our terror in separation. God understands! Jesus has said it as we do, "I feel abandoned. I despair."

And in his words is our salvation. Jesus has shared our pain. Jesus sits crouched in a corner alongside a young woman. As she cries out, "Why do I live?" he comforts her. Jesus sits alongside us when we are terrorized by life's unpredictability and pain.

"I am here with you," he tells us. "I know how you hurt. I understand your terror, your despair. You are not alone."

We, like the young woman, live in a world where events are not clear and explainable. Life is unfair because it is riddled with systems of sin and the interweavings of selfishness. Unfair. We feel alone and helpless, abandoned. But the fault line has been bridged. Jesus, the sinless one, cried out for us, "My God, why?" And God's answer soon came: You, my Son, will die so that all the others will know—nothing can separate the love of God from the people who cry for mercy and comfort. I am the Lord their God. I have sent you to bring them back—to me. Despair is not the end. It is the call for help. I am coming to save you. You live because I love you, and you are forever mine.

## To Consider

1. What events in the world seem especially unfair? When have I cried out to God and asked "why"?

2. In what situations in my personal life have I felt despair? When have I felt abandoned?

3. What times in my life did I feel God's love for me in spite of the difficulties I was going through?

4. When does human sin (either particular misdeeds or sin in general) cause suffering? Why do we have to be careful about saying that the actions of certain people or groups have caused suffering?

5. Why do we have to be careful about saying that God causes suffering, that suffering is God's will?

6. When have the following words from Paul's letter to the Romans brought comfort to us and to the Christians before us? "For I am convinced that neither death, nor life, nor angels, nor rulers, nor things present, nor things to come, nor powers, nor height, nor depth, nor anything else in all creation, will be able to separate us from the love of God in Christ Jesus our Lord" (Rom. 8:38-39).

# + Betrayal

Betrayal has stabbed everyone—
desertion by a friend
a secret made public
a co-worker taking advantage.
Someone we trusted let us down.
Jesus knew
    it was inevitable that
    one would turn from him,
    betray.
Jesus responded
    not with power and wrath
    but with a meal,
sharing himself
and calling them to serve.
We learn that Jesus
calls for more than justice.
He gives mercy
    and forgiveness and life.
He gives us a new Way.

*Walking the Way*
Fortress Press 1986
© Judith Mattison

# + Suffering

There is a limit
to my willingness to suffer.
I'm a comfort creature
and inclined to prefer to keep
    air conditioning and
    finer things at any cost.
Not extravagant, you understand.
Just comfortable.
Paul suggests that the Way
means openness to suffering—
    close to those who are sad
    standing with those in pain
    visiting the lonely, the disturbed
    sharing with the poor.
Uncomfortable.
It may mean sacrifice
    beyond my limit.
It may mean meeting Christ
    along the Way.

*Walking the Way*
Fortress Press 1986
© Judith Mattison

# + O Sacred Head, Now Wounded

O sacred head, now wounded,
With grief and shame weighed down,
Now scornfully surrounded
With thorns, thine only crown;
O sacred head, what glory,
What bliss till now was thine!
Yet, though despised and gory,
I joy to call thee mine.

How art thou pale with anguish,
With sore abuse and scorn;
How does that visage languish
Which once was bright as morn!
Thy grief and bitter Passion
Were all for sinners' gain;
Mine, mine was the transgression,
But thine the deadly pain.

What language shall I borrow
To thank thee, dearest friend,
For this thy dying sorrow,
Thy pity without end?
Oh, make me thine forever,
And should I fainting be,
Lord, let me never, never
Outlive my love to thee.

Lord, be my consolation;
Shield me when I must die;
Remind me of thy Passion
When my last hour draws nigh.
These eyes, new faith receiving,
From thee shall never move;
For he who dies believing
Dies safely in thy love.

*Attributed to Bernard of Clairvaux, 1091–1153;*
*trans. Paul Gerhardt, 1607–1676*

FIFTH WORD

"I am thirsty."

JOHN 19:28

# ✝ Our Partner on the Journey

**M**y friend Dyan and I had enjoyed lunch together one work day. As we walked the sidewalk alongside a busy city street on our way back to the office, suddenly my back tightened in a sharp, painful lower back spasm. I stood rigid, and then, in order to get some relief, I stooped down. It seemed to help momentarily. Dyan immediately stooped down beside me, asking if I was all right, offering to help.

We must have looked very strange to the motorists streaming by. Two grown women, stooped low to the ground for no apparent reason. My friend's compassion impressed me. In my pain, she did not stand above me. She came with me. It was as if Dyan said to me, "I am your partner in this journey." That simple act of solidarity remains etched in my memory of friendship. I felt comforted and reassured. Soon I could stand tall and move on once more.

Jesus dragged his cross along the streets of Jerusalem toward the hill of his demise, for the most part, alone. There were none close by to encourage him, to cheer him on. Rather, people jeered him; insults and disgust fell on his bleeding brow. Simon of Cyrene was enlisted to help carry the heavy cross. It was the only comfort Jesus received. Then, as he hung on the cross, his simple request for water was met with an offering of vinegar. Cruelty. Why? Why was it that Jesus had no partner on this journey to death, no compassionate friend? Psalm 69 paints the scene for us:

Insults have broken my heart,
    so that I am in despair.
I looked for pity, but there was none;
    and for comforters, but I found none.
They gave me poison for food,
    and for my thirst they gave me vinegar to drink.

(Ps. 69:20-21)

Why were people cruel when he called for water? Why was Jesus alone in his ultimate struggle? John records that Jesus received vinegar as a fulfillment of Scripture, a carrying out of the sixty-ninth psalm. What was God saying to us in the psalm and the vinegar? What is it that God would have us know in this unfolding drama of abandonment, abuse, and pain?

God would have us know that when Jesus asks for water, he is one of us. He is thirsty. He is human. He knows loneliness. He hurts, and he needs the power of God's love. Jesus is one of us.

Ours is a lonely journey at times. We're pilgrims, each of us. Our individuality is a miraculous gift, but it is also the source of a sense of isolation and loneliness that creeps into our hearts at times. We are born alone, and we die alone. No one can do it for us. As we take our talents and disabilities into the events of life, we alone experience the emotions and questions and mysteries of our particular journey. Occasionally we look up at a night sky and wonder about whether our life has any significance. Does what we do matter to anyone? We're lonely.

In our journey we encounter people and live in relationship. We may or may not have been physically beaten as Jesus was, but we have been scorned or criticized. We have been humiliated and overlooked. The journey among humankind is not smooth. Sometimes we wonder whether anybody really cares whether we are healthy or happy. We lose a job; we need encouragement. We're passed over on an invitation list; we need love. Our children disappoint us; we need support. We grow older; we need hope. Our friends are angry with us or someone spreads gossip about us that we cannot retrieve and counter; we hurt.

We also hurt physically. Our bodies weaken, our backs scream in pain. Of course. We are human and bodies weaken and die.

In our hurt or weakness or loneliness, when we wonder about the meaning of life, we thirst for the cool water of God's comfort, for the power of God's love. We are human beings and life overwhelms us. Who will understand? Who will comfort us, stoop down and be present with us? Who feels what we feel and offers assurance and help? God does.

But we ask, is God so far above us that we are insignificant and feel detached? Can so powerful a God really hear us cry, "I'm thirsty!"? How do we know God cares?

We know because the Scriptures tell us that God has gone before us on this journey we call life. God, in Jesus, walked the dusty road of insecurity—alone. Compassionately God touched the lepers; they were healed. God, born in Bethlehem as a human being, wept over the failing city of Jerusalem and over the death of his friend Lazarus. God knows what it is to grieve. God was betrayed by Judas, and his most loyal friends faded into the angry, screaming mob when he needed their encouragement and support.

God, in Jesus, was tempted by power and wealth. God knows our pain, our journey, because God in the person of Jesus has experienced the human struggle. Jesus is one of us. He has known our loneliness, our hurt. He has called out for God's love: "I am thirsty! I am thirsty!"

We might despair of life had Jesus not walked our human pathway. In his anguish and struggle we see our own trials and disappointments. God knew we needed full assurance of God's steadfast love for us. And so God in Jesus took the mantle of humanness, suffered and overcame it all—for us. For us to know that we are loved. We do not journey alone. In our times of deepest pain Jesus stoops down to be with us, saying, "I am your partner on this journey."

The story doesn't end there. All around us there are people who thirst for understanding or care, just as we do. "I thirst," pleads a homeless mother and her children. "I'm thirsty!" weeps the person with mental illness. "Stay with me," cries the lonely widow or the abused child or the man dying of cancer. "Please give me a cool drink of water," says the student who is harassed by the temptations of a drug culture. The cries of human beings ascend from the crosses of their lives every day.

Jesus hears. Jesus knows. And Jesus not only comforts people but also inspires us to carry the water of life to those who thirst. Because God in Jesus has loved us, we in turn walk with others on our common human journey. When pain strikes, we stoop to reassure and help them. Gently we touch the cool water of love to their lips. We show them by our actions that we have been loved back to life and want the same for all human beings, for them. With confidence we can offer them encouragement and hope: "Do not be afraid. Jesus understands. God is with you."

And so I say it to you today as well. My friend, if your journey is painful or frightening, if you feel lonely or weak, do not give up. Jesus has walked our journey toward death. He understands. The cool water of forgiveness is yours for the asking. My friend, Jesus says to you, "I am your partner on the journey of life." Take the hand of Jesus and drink from the living water of life.

## To Consider

1. Have I been delaying offering a cup of water to a person thirsty with need? What can I do?

2. We are born alone, and we die alone. When have I felt alone and lonesome? How have human relationships helped? How does my relationship with God help?

3. When in my life did I feel most needy? Did I know God was there?

4. What can I do when it doesn't feel as though God is with me?

5. How do we know God cares?

## + My Soul Thirsts

When is it that I thirst for God?
When I sigh for quiet
or weep for one who mourns,
when I tire of entertainment
or wonder about the world—
    life and death
    stars and creation.
I realize how seldom
I pray, or say to myself
"I have lived another day—
    how has it been?"
Longing for God is
yearning to be close to the Source,
    conscious of life
    and grateful,
living in harmony
    with nature and people,
    with God
    and the Way.

*Walking the Way*
Fortress Press 1986
© Judith Mattison

# + Where Cross the Crowded Ways of Life

Where cross the crowded ways of life,
Where sound the cries of race and clan,
Above the noise of selfish strife,
We hear your voice, O Son of Man.

In haunts of wretchedness and need,
On shadowed thresholds dark with fears,
From paths where hide the lures of greed,
We catch the vision of your tears.

From tender childhood's helplessness,
From human grief and burdened toil,
From famished souls, from sorrow's stress,
Your heart has never known recoil.

The cup of water giv'n for you
Still holds the freshness of your grace;
Yet long these multitudes to view
The strong compassion in your face.

*Frank M. North, 1850–1935, altered*

# + Lord, Whose Love in Humble Service

Lord, whose love in humble service
Bore the weight of human need,
Who upon the cross, forsaken,
Worked your mercy's perfect deed:
We, your servants bring the worship
Not of voice alone, but heart;
Consecrating to your purpose
Ev'ry gift which you impart.

Still your children wander homeless;
Still the hungry cry for bread;
Still the captives long for freedom;
Still in grief we mourn our dead.
As you, Lord, in deep compassion
Healed the sick and freed the soul,
By your Spirit send your power
To our world to make it whole.

As we worship, grant us vision,
Till your love's revealing light
In its height and depth and greatness
Dawns upon our quickened sight,
Making known the needs and burdens
Your compassion bids us bear,
Stirring us to ardent service,
Your abundant life to share.

*Albert F. Bayly, 1901–1984, altered*

SIXTH WORD

"*It is finished.*"

JOHN 19:30

# ✝ The Light of Accomplishment

In the beginning was the Word, and the Word was with God, and the Word was God." So begins John's Gospel, the good news of Jesus Christ. "And the Word became flesh and lived among us." Bone and muscle, brain and nerves, lungs and eyes and feet. The Word made into flesh and blood. God with us in the human struggle, in our struggle.

There was more to this human struggle than temptations in the wilderness or our commonplace notions of virtue wrestling with selfishness. When God took the form of Jesus the Christ, the battle was cosmic. Light entered into and shone in the darkness of sin, and, as John said in the beginning, "The darkness did not overcome it."

Throughout John's Gospel, Jesus announces that he has come to accomplish God's mission among people. "For I have come down from heaven, not to do my own will, but the will of him who sent me" (6:38).

Jesus claims his place, his authority: "I am the bread of life," "I am the good shepherd," "[I am] the living water," and then, "I am the light of the world." The light, John reminds us, has come to shine back the darkness. This light of the living God will meet our darkness and return us to the waiting arms of the God who loves us. Whether it is our grief or our disbelief, our anger with life's events or our discouragement or shame or guilt, the light of the world has come to bring us out of darkness.

And Jesus, the light, exposes our petty self-interest. The light of Jesus, the Word made flesh, exposes our personal and corporate sin. Against the light of the Savior, we see that sin is more than a list of misdeeds, or the sum of all our combined errors. Sin happens in spite of any goodness we may have. Sin is larger than all of us together. It is truly dark. Jesus alone can take control. Jesus exposes the truth: that we are too fragile, too weak to overcome our sin. Only Jesus, the Light of the world, can do that.

And now John brings us to the cross, nearing the very last of the struggle between light and darkness. Jesus is in charge. He asserts his authority. In the Garden of Gethsemane he does not wait to be arrested. Knowing all that is to befall him, he offers, "Whom do you seek?" From the cross he instructs John and his mother to care for each other. He fulfills Scripture by asking for something to drink. Jesus—bone, muscle, lungs, eyes, and feet in pain—is nonetheless in charge. The light shines, even on God's Friday as the sky grows dark.

Then he says, "It is finished," and he bows his head and gives up his spirit. Obediently, the Word-made-flesh gives up his spirit and dies.

What does it mean, to be "finished"? For Pilate and the government officials, having Jesus finished, over-and-done-with, was a relief. It was trouble enough to try to rule over a group of people with a culture totally unlike Rome. During Passover, one had to anticipate the possibility of demonstrations: all those people in town for their religious holiday. An uprising would bring nothing but bad press in Rome, and the ambitious Pilate didn't need another problem. Having Jesus "finished"—even at the risk of setting Barabbas free—would be a relief.

"Finished" for the religious leaders was a necessity if they intended to maintain control and power. Jesus was offensive to them, and having all those Jews following him was a threat. They wanted to return to business as usual: A Passover where they could charge high fees for sacrificial animals, no more fantastic tales of this man Jesus and his "healings." And they weren't about to put up with his claims of being the Son of God. Be done with him! Let the people calm down and get back to normal. The sooner he was finished, the better! The crowds would forget him after a while, once he was out of sight.

The disciples felt significantly different. "Finished" for them meant the end of a dream. For all the times Jesus had taken charge these last days or told them he was going to leave them, they chose not to believe him. Then, shocked by the dangerous realities of his arrest, trial, and crucifixion, the disciples cowered in the darkness. They had lost courage and had run away at the last moments. Their loss was more than flesh and blood. With Jesus went their hope of political victory or of the triumphant arrival of the awaited Messiah. Everything was ruined, wrecked! For the disciples, the struggle was lost. Darkness had won. It was finished.

For Jesus, "finished" was deeper. "It is finished" was God's Word spoken to a dark world by the child of light. Earlier Jesus had said to God, "I glorified you on earth by finishing the work that you gave me to do" (John 17:4). Jesus knew he had fulfilled his purpose even in death. To die was to obey, and he was satisfied. His whole life had had purpose, pointing always to God. His earlier cry, "Why have you forsaken me?" was erased as he voluntarily gave his life to God's great plan. "I have done what you ordained, God. It is finished. It is accomplished." No one *stole* life from him no matter what they may have thought. He *gave* it up because in the cosmic struggle of light and darkness it was necessary to die. The darkness did not overcome.

And when we encounter our darkness, how shall we be? When someone pronounces to you "malignant," do not yield hastily to despair, you of flesh and blood. The Light remains: Jesus, the Word-made-flesh. The Light will do battle with darkness. The rulers did not take life from him; rather he acted in obedience to the plan of God. The Light is still in charge.

Jesus says, "Do not let your hearts be troubled. Believe in God, believe also in me" (John 14:1). In our hour of death we may cry out, "My God, why have you forsaken me?" But the living Light answers, "I am with you always. You are mine. Come home. Your purpose is accomplished. It is finished."

When the struggles of darkness close around us, making ordinary days cloudy then black as midnight, how shall we meet the darkness? We are the ones who are too fragile and weak to overcome sin. How shall we meet suicide or death by a drunk driver? How shall we face the darkness of a dying child, the anxiety of our unforgiving personal regrets? How shall we live in a world so dark that we kill each other in the name of peace and ignore the silent cries of a lonely neighbor down the block and love things more than children?

How shall we meet the darkness? We too shall point always to God. It is our purpose. And we shall remember the Word-made-flesh on a cross. He told us to take care of each other. "You are the branches" (John 15:5). "I am the resurrection and the life" (John 11:25). "No one has greater love than this, to lay down one's life for one's friends" (John 15:13). "If the world hates you, be aware that it hated me before it hated you. . . . I have chosen you out of the world" (John 15:18-19). "You are the light of the world" (Matt. 5:14). To those of us immersed in the struggle of life's darkness, from the cross comes the Word made flesh. "Love one another as I have loved you" (John 15:12). "I go to prepare a place for you" (John 14:3). "It is finished" (John 19:30).

## To Consider

1. Do I sense that I have a purpose in life that is linked to God who created me?

2. Have there been times in my life when everything seemed ruined, but God worked things out for good?

3. How is it possible to see light in spite of darkness? What people that I know or have read about were able to do that? When am I able to do that?

4. Which of Jesus' "I am" statements speak most clearly to me: (I am) the bread of life, the good shepherd, the living water, the light of the world, the resurrection and the life?

5. When my life on earth is finished, what do I hope people will say about me? Will I have cast a shadow, or have I been linked to the Light?

## + We All Have Plans

We all have plans for our lives
    goals, dreams
    books to read
    projects to complete.
Some are accomplished.
Others are not
    and at times we are disappointed.
One task is never done—
the task of our perfecting ourselves
    being truly good,
    always loving,
    unselfish.
Try as we may, we always fail;
    sinners and disappointed.

Jesus came to the cross
led there by the promises of God,
    reluctant
yet ready to do what God required
in order to save us all.
His personal goals and dreams
had to be set aside
so that God's intention
to love us back to life
might be fulfilled.
His life
    and his death
had meaning, purpose:
God's will would be accomplished.
Jesus gave up the struggle against death,
satisfied that it was finished.

# ✠ Go to Dark Gethsemane

Go to dark Gethsemane,
All who feel the tempter's power;
Your Redeemer's conflict see.
Watch with him one bitter hour;
Turn not from his griefs away;
Learn from Jesus Christ to pray.

Follow to the judgment hall,
View the Lord of life arraigned;
Oh, the wormwood and the gall!
Oh, the pangs his soul sustained!
Shun not suffering, shame, or loss;
Learn from him to bear the cross.

Calvary's mournful mountain climb;
There adoring at his feet,
Mark that miracle of time,
God's own sacrifice complete.
"It is finished!" hear him cry;
Learn from Jesus Christ to die.

*James Montgomery, 1771–1854*

SEVENTH WORD

# "Father,
##     into your hands
##   I commend my spirit."

LUKE 23:46

# ✝ Letting Go

My friend Dr. John McClay reminded me of an old saying: "When I was in high school, some kids took cooking, some took woodworking, some took band, some took auto mechanics. I took control."

All of us like to take control of life. A poster about peace says, "Peace is not needing to know what will happen next." Few of us are free and secure enough to let go of our destiny and just live without trying to control the outcome. Now and then we experience the freedom of trusting God, but it may be rare.

Strangely enough, one of those times when I give up having to control my destiny is just before I slip under the power of anesthesia. I just let go. If I am going to survive, I will. If not, I'm in God's hands and that will be all right, too.

But do not suppose that I am always so trusting and free. On the whole, I am like many of us. I want to plan my life. Who of us hasn't dreamed and planned for retirement or Christmas or a picnic? We live in a goal-oriented society. We think in segments we call time. We organize our thoughts into patterns called logic. We even worship logic to the exclusion of experience. If it isn't logical, we don't take it seriously even if our own experience tells us otherwise. If we thought we could pull it off, we'd try to control the weather. We are very possessive of life and its events as if we had the power to manipulate nature and humankind. I laughed to read that in 1947, the Rocking F Ranch in Nevada had the audacity to formally lay claim to all water in any clouds that passed over it! (*The Book*

*of Days*, Donaldson, A & W Publishers, Inc., New York, 1979.)
The ranchers wanted to have control. I expect it didn't work.
We may not be like the ranchers, but the truth is, we all try
to bargain for control in our lives.

One of the seductive constructs by which many of us live is
that we in fact *do* have primary control over what happens.
This illusion is fed by the reality that we have many more
choices in our lives than do most of the world's people. We
are blessed with education that opens opportunity and creative
discovery to us. We have the choices that are allowed by suf-
ficient diet, mobility, and political freedom. We have choices
regarding health, artistic expression, and academic freedom.
Add to these significant choices, the millions of products from
which we can select, from laundry soap to fashions to soda
pop. It seems to us that we can choose our futures.

Until someone dies—a child, a friend, a famous philanthro-
pist, a spouse. Then our sense of control vanishes; our lives
are in disarray.

Also, we've lived long enough to discover that some people
seem to have an excess of what we call bad luck. Some families
experience one tragedy after another. We observe that life isn't
fair. The good die young, and sometimes the "bad guys" beat
the "good guys." We aren't in control.

And surely, sitting quietly in a valley between mountains
leaves us in awe of a world over which we have no ultimate
dominion. If we do not sense our frailty then, we certainly will
feel it when we walk through the ruins of buildings or forests
after a major storm. Control over life is an illusion. We live
by that myth a great deal, but it is only that—an idea, a myth,
an illusion.

When we feel shaky about life, we may turn to God for
security. However, sometimes that can be a convoluted attempt
to control our life and God too. "Dear God," we pray, "please
arrange life to suit us. Give us this. Restrict that. Change this
person. Punish that leader. Do it. Do it *my* way, Lord." Our
prayers are not an attempt to be in harmony with God's plans

for the world. Rather, they are an attempt to manipulate God to do what we desire. Please understand. I do not suggest that we should not pray. But when we do pray, "thy will be done," we are taking a risk. God *is* in control.

Perhaps we are most humorous as we try to control other people. A wife says to her husband, "I like you when you wear your navy blue suit." He replies, "I don't like navy blue." She returns, "But you look so nice. Why don't you wear it tonight?" Or a boyfriend tells his girlfriend, "I wish you wouldn't talk so much when you're nervous."

With our children we may be more subtle as we expect them to go to college or dress and cut their hair the way we prefer it. It's interesting to observe how youth find ways to declare their separate identity in spite of our history or rules. And more than one husband has left his navy blue suit in the closet despite the protests of his wife. Nervous girls aren't likely to cease talking just because they're told to. We do not control people, and the power struggles that develop when we try to do so are seldom worth the attempt. We may try to control others with anger, or we may try to please everyone by hiding our true feelings and being forever "nice." Neither method is likely to work.

Our attempts at controlling other people are signs of our human desire to be God. None of them works for long. Soon most people learn to ignore our angry outbursts or find ways of defeating them. Our withheld or "stuffed" feelings come out in one way or another, or else they play havoc with our insides and take control there. People don't necessarily change just because we want them to or because we are nice "people pleasers." In God's plan, people are intended to be who they are, to live out fully all the goodness they possess. Children are created unique with their own destinies, and hopefully they are allowed to develop as whole people. We are not intended to change others to suit ourselves or to poke fun at those unlike us. We are to help them be who they are created to be. Whether it is weather or people fulfilling our own goals, we are not in control.

In our battles regarding control, it is helpful to know that Jesus was faced with bargaining for control too. In the Garden of Gethsemane he prayed, "Father, if you are willing, remove this cup from me; yet, not my will but yours be done" (Luke 22:42). Was he not like us, praying and hoping he would not have to die, that he could control his destiny? Did he not yearn to change the story, to control the people around him in order to save himself? "Remove this cup from me." He struggled with his reality just as we do. He didn't want to die.

Then on the cross he was fully human. He thirsted, he expressed concern for his mother and friend, he was upset with God for leaving him. He fought to live and struggled to forgive. Then in a moment of grandeur and simplicity, he let go. "Father, into your hands I commend my spirit."

Jesus did what we must do. He gave his life back to the one who gives each of us life and breath and hope. Into God's hands he gave his whole being.

The great human quest of folly is to try to control God or to be God. We seek to please God with prayer or deeds. We try to manipulate God in order to live longer or be rid of pain and problems or be more prosperous. This is our self-worship, deciding we know what's best for ourselves and all others. We defy God's power by exerting our own. We deny God's power over life by not asking for help. We pretend we are God by trying to control others. And the ultimate control issue for us is our attempt to deny or control the hour of our death.

Turn your eyes upon Jesus today. He who had the power of God chose not to try to control. Rather, as a human being, he let go. He left his destiny in the hands of the Creator, who promises to love us eternally. Jesus knew what we long to believe: God loves us beyond our understanding or deserving. God is in control, and that is *good*! We pray with our Lord Jesus today, "Father, into your hands I commend my spirit."

# To Consider

1. What person or people in my life do I attempt to control or manipulate? Do I use promises, persuasion, being nice, or anger? Do they work?

2. When did I think I had control of a situation or person but didn't? What happened?

3. What should I do when I desperately want things my own way? For which issues is having my own way really important to me, and for which ones doesn't it matter?

4. What happens when several people want things their own way?

5. When is it hardest to let go?

# + Temptation

Temptation goes beyond sweets
    self-interest
    greed and lust.
My greatest temptation
    is to believe
I don't need God.
I'm good at problem-solving,
few situations overwhelm me.
We live comfortably.
I've recovered from illness,
and learned to live with pain.
The way it looks
I can live a good life
    until I die.
Until I die!
    There it is . . .
I have no ultimate control.
You alone are God.
Show me your Way.

*Walking the Way*
Fortress Press 1986
© Judith Mattison

## + Power

We try to control life
with well-constructed plans
    investments
    weather reports
and appeals to God
    when all else fails.
Pilate thought he had power, too.
Pilate and we are wrong.
We have only the power
    which God allows—
and freedom to respond,
    but not to direct God,
the privilege of enjoying life
but not of numbering our days.
Pilate and the others—we—
    crucified Jesus
a power play,
doomed to fail
so that we might live.

*Walking the Way*
Fortress Press 1986
© Judith Mattison

## + Darkness

From a distance of centuries
I stand observing
as darkness rolls over the sun
and God is gone.
Despair.
Innocence destroyed.
Surely this scene
is reenacted again and again.
We live in darkness
   and mourn the light
giving up on life
and doubting the Promise.
His last words were
   "Father, into thy hands."
Jesus never abandoned God.
Lord, in our darkest hours
reach your hand to ours
and lead us in your Way
to hope.

*Walking the Way*
Fortress Press 1986
© Judith Mattison

## + Make Me a Captive, Lord

Make me a captive, Lord,
   And then I shall be free;
Force me to render up my sword,
   And I shall conqueror be.
I sink in life's alarms
   When by myself I stand;
Imprison me within thine arms,
   And strong shall be my hand.

My heart is weak and poor
   Until it master find;
It has no spring of action sure,
   It varies with the wind.
It cannot freely move
   Till thou has wrought its chain;
Enslave it with thy matchless love,
   And deathless it shall reign.

My power is faint and low
   Till I have learned to serve;
It wants the needed fire to glow,
   It wants the breeze to nerve;
It cannot drive the world
   Until itself be driven;
Its flag can only be unfurled
   When thou shalt breathe from heaven.

My will is not my own
   Till thou hast made it thine;
If it would reach a monarch's throne
   It must its crown resign;
It only stands unbent
   Amid the clashing strife,
When on thy bosom it has leant
   And found in thee its life. Amen.

*George Matheson, 1842–1906*

## + Beneath the Cross of Jesus

Beneath the cross of Jesus I long to take my stand;
The shadow of a mighty rock within a weary land,
A home within the wilderness, a rest upon the way,
From the burning of the noontide heat and burdens of the day.

Upon the cross of Jesus, my eye at times can see
The very dying form of one who suffered there for me.
And from my contrite heart, with tears, two wonders I confess:
The wonder of his glorious love and my unworthiness.

I take, O cross, your shadow for my abiding place;
I ask no other sunshine than the sunshine of his face;
Content to let the world go by, to know no gain nor loss,
My sinful self my only shame, my glory all, the cross.

*Elizabeth C. Clephane, 1830–1869*

# ✝ A Devotional Response to Jesus' Last Words

We have heard the voice of Jesus from the cross, showing and sharing with us what it means to struggle with death. It will not be enough to set those words and that scene aside, eager to get to Easter and forget the past. We have journeyed with Jesus' followers to Calvary, and we have anguished with Jesus on the cross. We must now wait and walk yet one journey more. It is not over yet. It is only Saturday.

If we would wrestle with faith, we must place ourselves into the lives of those who were present at the time of the crucifixion. What did they experience? How does the crucifixion relate to our lives? And how do Jesus' words enlighten their faith struggle and ours?

We cannot avoid Jesus' pain and his cries for water. Our culture is one of optimism. Douglas John Hall, in his book, *Lighten Our Darkness*, characterizes our cultural mindset as "officially optimistic." He suggests that to be realistic is often branded as a negative or pessimistic outlook. Many of us have subscribed to that thinking, whether in economic or personal matters. Optimism is a helpful approach to some aspects of life, but it does not have real substance and depth. Cynicism is a way of writing off life without feeling its impact. Optimism can do the same by avoiding the pain and struggle of life. Optimism and positive thinking, while they can be helpful, pale in the light of the intensity of the death of God, the death of Jesus. Optimism is not adequate in the face of death.

Optimism calls us to brush lightly over the complexities of life and death, to clean off and polish the cross for our altars without looking at and experiencing the agonizing spectacle of a dead Lord. When his friends removed Jesus from the cross, surely they got blood on their hands. One does not hastily wash away the odor and color of one's friend's blood. It may be tempting to envision our reunion with Jesus in Paradise (which he promised the thief) without coming to terms with the suffering and sacrifice which are necessary before that reunion. We must not close our eyes to the sight and sound of Jesus dying, pleading for water. Our lives and our deaths will and do experience emptiness, thirst, and pain before we experience resurrection and reunion. Optimism is a weak combatant with death.

On our Saturday we must remember that Jesus died in pain, and we cannot move hastily by him. We remember his words, "I am thirsty." We, too, will thirst for righteousness and for love and companionship on our journey. We thirst for meaning: Why was I born? Why do I struggle? Jesus reminds us that he understands and that God thirsts for relationship with us at all times. This is our *hope*. It is not shallow optimism. Hoping for God's companionship and forgiveness in the midst of our honest pain is the way of the cross.

Saturday was filled with grief and fear for the disciples. My friend Joy has described grief as a dead-weight agony in the stomach, and so it is. The disciples ran from Good Friday and hid themselves away not only because they were afraid but also because they were struggling with an incomprehensible loss. Jesus, the person, was gone. Forever. In darkness and tears, they took him from the cross. How lonely! And with his death went their dreams—dreams of a Messiah, dreams of a better world, and the persistent belief that Jesus had power over all things. The disciples wanted to believe Jesus was God, but his dying struck them across the face with a decided No! He died. He was gone. The dream and the life were over.

As with suffering and dying, one does not hastily move through grief and loss. Bit by bit one acknowledges sad moments, bittersweet memories, broken dreams. Who would lead them now? they wondered. When Jesus said, "It is finished," they heard despair more than the voice of accomplishment. The disciples heard his cries. They couldn't deny his pain. He bled in their arms. They wept, for it was lonely without him. They didn't know the future or have perspective on God's ultimate plan. They despaired.

We, too, must pause to allow grief and loss to be processed. We have discovered that to rush headlong into Easter and "better times" does not remove unexpected stabs of grief and loss. At best it only delays the necessary expression of our sadness. It will not be finished until we acknowledge all the circumstances and nuances of our losses. We are only human. We will not sidestep grief. Grief is a cross that we, too, will carry until, at last, it is finished when we have met God in our pain and allowed God to comfort and change us. Our lives will not be finished until we have fully experienced all that life has brought us, grief included. Then we commend our spirit into the compassionate hands of the one who creates and sustains us.

On God's Friday evil won. We hate that thought, that evil's power overcame the Son of God, the hope of all people for all time. But it is true. It was a cold and bitter moment when "The King of the Jews" was taken from his cross and carried away. Our optimism scurries up and faintly pleads that surely we are mistaken. God doesn't die!

Today it is the same. We try to deny the existence and power of evil. We do it all the time. "Surely you are mistaken." Our language dilutes the truth as we refer to misguided people or unfortunate circumstances. Our minds close out the manifestations of evil—beaten children and wives, racial supremacists, images of the Holocaust, or a videotape of dead war victims. We want to deny it, but evil does win. Our fairy tales have encapsulated evil in wolves and beasts and stepmothers. We

81

try to confine our awareness of evil in the same way, by projecting evil onto a few identifiable people. Then we can dismiss it as manageable. But on Good Friday, evil ran roughshod. It overcame all the world. In the persons of politicians and religious leaders, the military and cowardly friends, evil rose up and extinguished the Light of the world. Evil won. Death won. Optimism was worthless. "My God, why have you forsaken me?" My God, why have you forsaken us? Saturday was despair. There was thirst and blood and despair. There was no room for denial. The finality of death was real.

We cannot take Jesus from the cross without getting blood on our hands. We must carry the body, stumbling through an evil and inhospitable world in which we experience betrayal like his, and losses, physical pain, suffering, and despair. Saturday is the place where we live every day. We live in the tomb.

We have the promise of Easter. But we have not Easter yet. We live, as Dietrich Bonhoeffer says, in the penultimate moment. Our tomb is constructed of the denial of death and evil. It is dug into the side of a hill called despair. We prefer pretending that life is under our control rather than acknowledging that we are powerless against sin and death.

Our tomb is dark, dark for we fear suffering and avoid sacrifice. We have not understood why Jesus thirsted and suffered, despaired and died. We are trapped in a tomb of human self-sufficiency and fear of death, and our optimism is too fragile to roll the stone away. Locked into ourselves, we have no power. We are both executioner and victim, powerless to find the light.

From the cross we heard the only words which can save us. "Father, forgive them." Forgive our apathy amidst evil and our fear of sacrificial suffering. Forgive our insensitivity to others and our attempts at controlling life.

Then, again, his voice, "Father, into your hands I commend my spirit." Father, we say, I will face it. I will confront my own frail humanity and the cross of my inevitable death. I am powerless. I need God. I need Jesus to save me from death. "Into your hands I commend *my* spirit."

Only then does the huge stone begin to move so that the light of Easter morning is revealed. God meets us *in our darkness*. The darkness is overcome. Only then will Saturday be over.

## To Consider

1. Do we tend to rush too soon through the pain of Good Friday to the joy of Easter? What happens when evil and suffering are passed over too quickly?

2. What happens when people who are coming out of traumatic situations don't grieve, when they don't let themselves feel the weight of the terrible experiences they went through?

3. How does Jesus' crucifixion relate to my life? Is it significant primarily because through it I am forgiven of all my sin, or can I see other meanings as well?

4. Which of the seven last words of Christ means the most to me now? During what occasions might his other words speak to me?

5. Why is the admission of our powerlessness a first step out of the darkness toward meeting God, toward Easter?

# + O Love That Will Not Let Me Go

O Love that will not let me go,
I rest my weary soul in thee;
I give thee back the life I owe,
That in thine ocean depths its flow
May richer, fuller be.

O Light that followest all my way,
I yield my flick'ring torch to thee;
My heart restores its borrowed ray,
That in thy sunshine's blaze its day
May brighter, fairer be.

O Joy that seekest me through pain,
I cannot close my heart to thee;
I trace the rainbow through the rain
And feel the promise is not vain
That morn shall tearless be.

O Cross that liftest up my head,
I dare not ask to fly from thee;
I lay in dust life's glory dead,
And from the ground there blossoms red
Life that shall endless be.

*George Matheson, 1842–1906, altered*